Let's Learn About…
GOATS
By: Breanne Sartori

All Rights Reserved. No part of this publication may be reproduced in any form or by any means, including scanning, photocopying, or otherwise without prior written permission of the copyright holder. Copyright © 2014

Introduction

You probably think of goats as cute white animals that look like sheep with horns. But did you know that goats actually come in a lot of different sizes and colours and some of them look really strange! They are really smart animals and can quickly form good (or bad) habits.

What Goats Look Like

Goats can be big or small, have curly, straight, long or short hair and come in lots of different colours! They all have two horns on their head and a small tail. Even their eyes come in lots of different colours!

Size

Some goats are really tiny and others are huge. The smallest breed of goat only weighs 20 pounds. The biggest is about 250 pounds! They can also grow to be over 4 feet tall.

Horns

Most goats have horns and horns are the easiest way to tell if it's a goat instead of a sheep! Some species naturally don't have horns though. You know the stuff that our fingernails are made of? It's called keratin and it's also what goat horns are made of!

Fur

Goat fur comes in all sorts of colours – brown, black, white, tan, red or even yellow. Some have spots or are multiple colours! Some goats are bred especially for their fur, like cashmere and angora goats. Have you heard of those materials?

Eyes

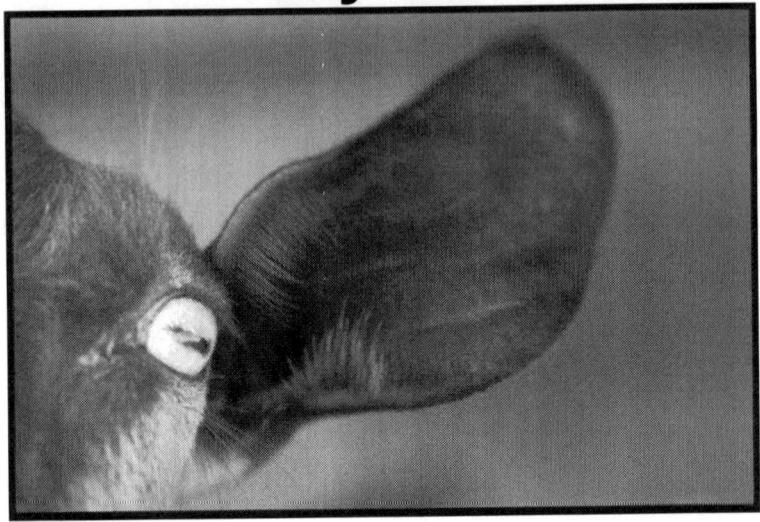

Just like their fur, goat's eyes can come in many different colours. Most have yellow or brown eyes though. They are able to see in the dark really well and often eat at night. Strangely, when it's very bright, the pupils of their eyes become rectangles!

Where Goats Live

Goats are originally from Asia and Europe, but now they can be found anywhere! Goats in the wild prefer to live in places that are quite barren, which means there aren't many plants. A lot of goats like to live in the mountains or other rocky places.

Climbing

Did you know that goats are really good climbers? They have to be to live in the mountains! Their hooves are really good for climbing along rocks. Goats can easily jump and run across rocky places too!

What Goats Eat

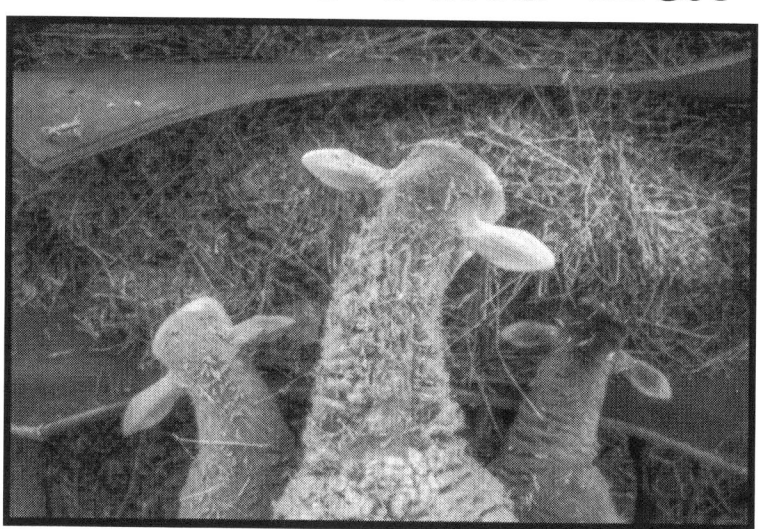

Goats love grass! In fact, for most of the time it's all they eat! Goats are grazing animals which means they spend a lot of time eating. They will also eat fruit, weeds, shrubs and even woody plants.

Stomach

Goats are ruminants, just like cows. This means that they have four stomachs! Their digestive system never stops working and it can take between 11 and 15 hours for food to digest. They also need to re-chew food that they've already eaten!

Herds

Goats are social animals and live in herds. Unlike sheep though, it's very hard to herd goats! They communicate with each other by bleating, which is what the "baa" sound is called. Goats bleat when they are hungry, stressed or to call to each other.

Baby Goats

Did you know goats can have twins? They can even have triplets! Baby goats, like most animals, feed on their mother's milk when they are young. They weigh about 6 pounds when they are born and can grow quickly.

Breeding

Goats don't have a certain breeding season – they breed whenever they want! They usually breed depending on the climate though, using the length of the day as a guide. When the female gets pregnant, it will be another 5 months before her baby is born.

The Life of a Goat

Baby goats grow up very quickly! They are able to eat solid food after only 8 weeks. They are fully mature and able to have their own babies at 6 months! Most goats will live for 10 years but some will live a little longer.

Predators

It can be very dangerous for goats! There are a lot of natural predators in the wild. Leopards, tigers, mountain lions, wolves and snakes will all eat goats. Even goats on farms aren't always safe from wolves.

Defending Themselves

Poor goats! They don't have a very good ability to defend themselves. Their horns can be used to fight off predators, but they aren't always long enough to be useful. Most have to use their ability to run and jump across the rocky landscape to escape!

Domesticated Goat

Domesticated goats aren't really a separate species. It just refers to the types of goats that are bred for milk, meat and their fur. Most are descended from the Bezoar goat, species of wild goat from the Middle East.

Fainting Goat

The fainting goat is possibly the strangest species of goat. It's quite rare and is from the area around Tennessee in the United States. But what makes them interesting is that they actually do faint! They topple over and then get back up and continue grazing until it happens again!

Anglo-Nubian Goat

The Anglo-Nubian goat is a domestic goat that is bred for it's milk. Because there is a high content of fat in their milk, their milk is good for making cheese. They are originally from the United Kingdom, but are bred all over the world.

Mountain Goat

Mountain goats are a breed of goat that is found in the wild. As you probably guessed, it lives in the mountains and other rocky places. They are much bigger than domestic goats, but they aren't actually true goats! They have thick fur to keep them warm high up in the cold mountains.

Cashmere Goat

The cashmere goat is a popular goat for farmers to breed. It's fleece is very popular and can be very expensive to buy. They are shaved once every year and can produce over 2 pounds of cashmere!

Made in the USA
Lexington, KY
21 October 2015